SO-FBR-667

ISBN 1-877038-68-7

Profile The Market

by

Jordan Kelly

Software Publications

Profile The Market

Author: Jordan Kelly

Editor: Penelope Johnson

ISBN: 1-877038-68-7

Disclaimer

Publishers – Software Publications Pty Ltd (ABN 75 078 026 150)

Head Office – Sydney
Unit 10, 171 Gibbes Street
Chatswood NSW 2067
Australia

Web Address
www.softwarepublications.com

Branches

Adelaide, Brisbane, Melbourne, Perth and Auckland

TABLE OF CONTENTS

What Is Marketing?

What Are You Marketing?

Segmenting The Overall Market

Identifying Your Target Markets

Developing A Positioning Strategy

Putting It All Together

Section 1:
What is Marketing?

Marketing in Today's Commercial Environment

'Marketing' has been a popular buzzword for several decades now. As a result, it's become one of the most elastic words in the English language. Mostly it has been used in the falsely limited context of 'promotion' or 'sales'. Now is a good time to put paid to such a limited notion of the powerful and all-encompassing discipline of marketing.

In essence, marketing is all about knowing your customer so well that the product or service you develop — the way you price it, package it, distribute or deliver it, and communicate its benefits — makes the sales process simply the full stop at the end of the sentence.

A marketing-oriented approach places the emphasis on the needs and wants of the customer, and the satisfaction of those desires through the 'bundle of benefits' represented by the product, service or concept being marketed.

By contrast, the sales-oriented approach places the emphasis on the product (or service, or concept) itself, along with its features. It's an increasingly outdated approach in which, essentially, an organisation decides for itself what it wishes to produce, and then goes about selling it the best way it can.

A marketing-driven organisation, however, identifies the needs and wants of its desired target market and then sets about producing products or developing services that will satisfy the desires of such a customer base.

Whether the term 'marketing' is used in its strictly commercial sense (which is, of course, its most common form of usage), or employed in a broader, non-commercial context, it's a discipline revolving around one central concept — the 'target market'.

Increasingly, even the most stubborn, die-hard 'mass marketers' are turning to 'target marketing' strategies, as today's consumer marketplace continually fragments itself according to the wants and needs of an ever-evolving, ever-demanding society.

In fact, in today's consumer marketplace, an increasing proportion of product manufacturers and service providers attain their commercial success through 'niche marketing', an even more finely-honed and selective form of target marketing.

The progressive corporation of the third millennium dedicates its entire existence to the identification, constant reassessment, and satisfaction of customers, in a precisely pinpointed and well-understood target market.

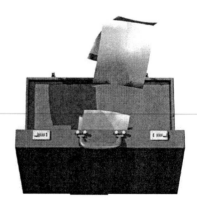

4

The Role of Market Segmentation, Target Market Selection and Competitive Positioning in Successful Marketing

Please Note: The terms 'company' and 'organisation' are used interchangeably throughout this textbook. The term 'organisation' is used as a reminder that the application of 'marketing' is not limited to commercial products and services.

Effective marketing requires an in-depth, detailed and up-to-the-minute understanding of an organisation's target market or markets.

One of the first and most critical tasks in preparing a marketing strategy is the identification and analysis of those segments of an organisation's overall marketplace, which it can most appropriately and profitably service.

Companies select target markets on which to concentrate their efforts for any or all of the following reasons:

- The nature and needs of the overall marketplace vary too much to effectively service the total market.

- A competitor or competitors are servicing part or all of the market and the organisation either wishes to avoid over-serviced segments, or to differentiate its offering within the various segments of the marketplace.

- The organisation wishes to specialise in satisfying the needs of a certain segment of the overall marketplace.

Thus, it is critical for a company's marketers to correctly identify its overall marketplace; determine how to 'segment' it into profitably serviceable sectors; select the most strategic of these sectors; and decide on the way in which its offering will be 'positioned' against those of its competitors. This provides the foundation for the next phases in the total marketing effort.

The equally critical objective of this initial, and cornerstone, phase is the direction and parameters it sets for obtaining an in-depth knowledge, or 'profile', of the company's target markets.

An organisation that has accurately segmented its market, strategically selected its target segments, and obtained an in-depth understanding of the consumers comprising these target markets, will have laid solid foundations for the success of its marketing strategy.

Discussion Exercise (Group):

Discuss the increasing need for clear selection of target markets in today's marketing environment.

Your Challenge (Individual):

Select a specific consumer product manufacturing corporation or service firm for this exercise. Refer to the preceding text to review the various reasons an organisation may have for selecting a target market strategy (as opposed to mass marketing). Provide a written outline of your views as to why your selected organisation has chosen a targeted marketing approach.

_____

_____

_____

_____

_____

_____

_____

_____

_____

Section 2:
What Are You Marketing?

Different Types of Marketing

There are many different products, services and concepts that can be marketed. As such, it can be said that there are many 'types' of marketing.

Here are some examples: product marketing, services marketing, event marketing, cause marketing (e.g. environmental marketing), political marketing, personality marketing, educational marketing, travel marketing, franchise marketing, non-profit marketing, idea or concept marketing and change or advocate marketing.

Some organisations engage in multiple types of marketing. For example, Subway Sandwiches markets sandwiches and other food and beverage items, but it also markets franchises. The RSPCA markets for donors, but it also engages in change or advocate marketing, endeavouring to bring about community awareness of animal welfare issues.

Some organisations are involved in different strata of marketing, e.g. business-to-business marketing, business-to-Government marketing, Government-to-citizen marketing and industrial marketing.

Still other organisations are engaged in multiple types of marketing within various different marketplaces, or marketplace strata.

Exercise (Group):

Identify current, real-world examples of:

- ◆ Business-to-business marketing

_____

_____

_____

- ◆ Government-to-citizen marketing

_____

_____

_____

- ◆ Environmental marketing

_____

_____

_____

Section 3: Segmenting the Overall Market

Identifying Your Overall Market

> For the purposes of our study we will concentrate, for the most part, on the marketing of commercial products and services

What is a 'market'?

A market comprises everyone who is either a current or potential future buyer of a product or service.

However, most companies find such a definition far too broad. Trying to cater for everyone who would ever conceivably buy their offering would make almost every element of the marketing mix unwieldy (e.g. distribution and promotion).

The decisions the company might make with regard to some elements of the marketing mix may work for a part of the market, but may well alienate other parts of the market.

A hypothetical example of this would be a shampoo manufacturer who, with one brand and one 'positioning', tries to appeal to a market made up of some consumers who want a cost-effective, 'family' shampoo (a supermarket brand), some who want a gentle, 'everyday' shampoo and are prepared to pay a 'salon' level price, and yet others who see their hair care products almost in the realm of the pharmaceutical, to be recommended strictly by a knowledgeable professional.

In this example, each consumer 'type' has widely varying functional and emotional needs. And so it is with most products and services, particularly in the consumer marketplace.

Identifying the overall market is, however, the starting point for the segmentation process, and provides the overall 'set' from which the target 'subsets', or segments, will be chosen.

Identifying the market and then working through its segmentation can be viewed as a funnelling process — the total group of all potential buyers is dropped in the top, and then progressively funnelled down through the different selection criteria, until the group with the most ideal customer attributes pops out the bottom.

So to start with, who represents the overall market for a product or service?

The overall market is all persons or organisations with needs or wants which your product or service could potentially satisfy, and who have the buying power and, potentially, the will to purchase your product or service.

In very general terms, an organisation could determine its overall — or 'starting point' — market, as those parties who have an awareness of the product or service category, a sufficient knowledge and appreciation of the benefits provided by that product or service, access to a point of purchase for the product or service, the ability to use the product or service, and the capacity to pay for the product or service.

Developing A Broad Vision

Developing a broad vision of the market provides the framework for assessing general market demand.

Even within the same industry, different companies' definitions of their overall marketplace can vary dramatically. Some companies take an extremely broad view of their marketplace. Others take a far narrower view of their overall market.

To develop a broad vision, the marketer must step back from the inevitable focus on the product or service, or intended product or service, and view the offering as a bundle of benefits capable of satisfying the specific needs or wants of a particular group of people or organisations.

A strong and clear *company mission* is of great assistance in developing an initial broad — and even visionary — definition of a company's overall market.

The legendary success of Aussie Home Loans emanated from the vision of its founder John Symond, who saw his overall marketplace as extending to any Australian resident his company could empower to live the Great Australian Dream of owning their own home. This also included anyone who they could help 'Get Home Sooner' by reducing the time span of existing or potential new mortgages. In other words, Symond did not view his market simply as 'Australian residents seeking mortgage finance'.

Beginning with such a broad view of its market, Aussie Home Loans was no doubt able to ultimately identify a greater range of market segments at which to target its mortgage products.

Apple provides a more global example of a corporation taking a broad view of its market, and using its company mission to generate that viewpoint.

With its vision of a new generation of PC users proficient in Apple technology by the time they leave high school, Apple became a force in schools and broadened its market past what might have been a more narrow and shorter-range perspective.

In other words, it could have simply gone after the age groups with the immediate discretionary dollars, but it viewed its market through long-range vision.

Ultimately, taking an initial broad market vision not only helped both these companies identify strategic market segments to target, it also helped them identify a greater number of them.

The key is, firstly, to begin with an unrestricted view of the market, and secondly, to anticipate its potential or future wants and needs — to 'think for the market'. Or, put another way, to 'do the market's thinking for it'.

Exercise (Group) :
Identify and discuss the visions of both a global, and a local, company.

_____

_____

_____

_____

_____

_____

_____

_____

_____

What Business Are You In?

Another approach to ensure an organisation commences the marketing process with a sufficiently broad view of its overall marketplace is to not restrict its view of its potential customers as those seeking its specific product or service, but to also include buyers of any other product or service that could be substituted for the marketer's product or service.

For example, a pizza chain could see itself as being in the *pizza business*. Alternatively, it could see itself as being in the *fast food business*. Yet more broadly still, it could see itself as being in the *convenient meal solutions* business.

Each different viewpoint throws a different perspective on its marketplace. Note that the broadest market definition — i.e. the *convenient meal solutions* marketplace — offers the greatest potential for market segmentation and, therefore, the greatest number of potential target markets.

It is important to again point out that there is no conflict between taking a broad — even 'mass market' — approach to the identification of an organisation's overall market. It is such visionary and 'outside the square' thinking that helps pinpoint potentially lucrative target markets.

A broad initial perspective helps identify both competitive threats and opportunities which may well come from outside a more narrowly defined marketplace, eroding the market share of companies who fail to recognise the broader range of options available to its customers in satisfying their needs.

A good starting point is for marketers to re-define and view their product or service as a '**bundle of benefits**' rather than as a tangible item. In other words, the set of benefits a consumer purchasing the product or service will derive from it.

This helps the marketer see the offering from the consumer's perspective, and also helps to identify all groups who would potentially benefit from the use of the product or service in question.

Understanding the scope of the company's total market also helps marketers position the organisation for any potential growth opportunities. And again, the breadth of growth opportunities it is able to capitalise on will be proportionate to how broad and insightful its view of its overall marketplace is.

Horizontal and Vertical Markets

A broad perspective of the company's overall market is instrumental, also, in identifying horizontal and vertical integration opportunities.

Markets can be expanded either '**horizontally**' or '**vertically**', often referred to as '**vertical integration**' or '**horizontal integration**'.

By way of example, Coca Cola Amatil could be said to have carried out a certain type of vertical integration within its marketplace when it began placing vending machines in office workplaces. Berri Ltd (more widely known by its old name, Berri Fruit Juices) could be said to have expanded its market horizontally by entering the sports drinks market with its IsoSport and Edge brands.

> **Vertical Integration** involves the organisation gaining control of additional 'links' in the production or distribution 'chain'. **Horizontal Integration** is the expansion of the organisation's product or services portfolio, and/or the organisation's expansion into other markets.

As a marketer, starting with a clear understanding of your company's vision or mission, an equally clear understanding of your product or service as a package of 'benefits', and a broad and forward-thinking view of your overall marketplace, will help you more accurately identify a greater range of potentially profitable target markets, along with future growth opportunities.

Exercise (Group):

Select any consumer product corporation within the national marketplace. Discuss the 'business it is in'. Determine a narrow, product-based definition of its overall market. Then determine a broad, mission-based or needs-based market definition.

_____

_____

_____

_____

_____

_____

_____

_____

_____

_____

_____

_____

_____

_____

_____

_____

_____

_____

Determining Segmentation Criteria Relevant to the Product, Service or Concept You Are Marketing

To effectively segment an overall market into the most potentially profitable target markets, marketers need to ensure each identified segment possesses the 'qualifiers' listed below. How important each qualifier is in relation to another will depend upon many factors unique to your organisation, your offering and your own marketing mix-related capacities.

Criteria — The Marketer's Perspective

All segments selected for consideration as target markets should be:

1) Measurable

A market segment must be readily measurable — firstly in terms of its size, and secondly in terms of the purchasing power of the customers it represents. These two factors combined are a basic determinant of the segment's profitability.

The need for measurability, of course, throws up one further critical criterion. And that is that useful statistical data or other information must be available to help assess the market segment. It is an unsound practice to decide to segment a market on bases for which no reliable data is obtainable.

2) Identifiable

Segments should be readily identifiable to the extent that they can be given strategic titles relevant to the industry or its product e.g. '18 to 35s', 'fun seekers', 'cola die-hards', 'appearance conscious'. (We will discuss this in the section *Segment Descriptors Used in Consumer Marketing*.)

16   © Jordan Kelly

3)   Accessible

A market segment should be accessible through existing or practical distribution channels, as well as existing or practical marketing communications vehicles.

4)   Substantial

Obviously, a segment must be of a sufficient size to be profitable. Clearly this will differ widely for different industries and different products or services but, in general terms, an organisation should target the market segment or segments comprising the largest possible group reachable with a customised marketing mix.

5)   Distinguishable

Any given market segment should differ in its response to the benefits package, marketing mix, marketing messages and other promotional stimuli substantially to that of other market segments. The absence of such differentiation renders a tailored marketing program invalid.

6)   'Homogenous'

On the other hand, a market should be segmented such that the members within any given segment are likely to respond to the benefits package, marketing mix, marketing messages and other promotional stimuli as similarly as possible.

7)   Stable

A segment, its members, and the predictability of their behaviour relevant to the organisation's product or service, should be reasonably and demonstrably stable on past statistics.

8) Practical to Service

A market segment should not exceed an organisation's ability to service it practically and profitably.

The above market segmentation criteria are based on considerations from the *marketer's* perspective. However, when segmenting a market and then selecting target markets from those segments, there are several other considerations to be made from a higher-level *organisational* viewpoint.

Criteria — The Organisational Perspective

These criteria include but are not limited to:

1) Synergy with Organisational Growth Objectives

A segment must, through careful research, demonstrate its potential growth as being in line with the organisation's general growth objectives and expansion strategies.

For example, a company might be looking to consolidate after entry into a market segment. It would therefore not be strategic to select a market segment growing at such a rate that it would require a significant ongoing capital injection to enable the company to maintain its foothold against competitors.

Equally, it would not be strategic for an organisation with the objective of rapid growth to enter a market segment within an otherwise mature market. Whilst its competitive positioning and a savvy marketing mix may gain it a worthwhile market for its product, it is still unlikely to realise the growth rate of a rapidly expanding market segment.

2)   Consistency with Corporate Image

An organisation might or might not maintain a specific image. This image might or might not have relevance to the decision to enter a specific market segment.

For example, a company bearing a designer's name might not wish to enter a particular market segment the characteristics of which clash with its overall corporate image, even though the market segment may offer significant potential for its product.

Developing the market mix (e.g. distribution channel and promotional program) for the market segment in question would mean diverging from the marketing component of its established image in a highly visible way.

However, this might not be a consideration for, say, a large consumer products manufacturer with a portfolio of existing brands spanning a range of market categories and 'images'.

3)   Competitors' Strategies

A market segment that is already being serviced by a key competitor, several key competitors, or a large number of general competitors, might not represent a strategic opportunity for an organisation.

Whilst such a segment might, for example, represent strong market growth or other expansion opportunities, the presence of significant competition in the marketplace could require ongoing significant investment in product improvement, differentiation and promotion of the organisation's competitive positioning. The presence of such competition might also force continued line extension or vertical or horizontal market growth, for which the organisation might be unprepared.

Closely related to this consideration, is whether or not the organisation possesses resources and skills superior to that of the competition in order that it can, with substance, promote a superior offering to the members of this market segment.

Finally, in this category of consideration is whether or not the organisation's entry into that market segment will increase the product choice of that segment to the extent that it becomes too much of a 'buyer's market'.

4) Cost of Entry

The cost of entry into a market segment may render an otherwise attractive market non-viable, or at least, not strategic in terms of the organisation's greater goals and objectives.

The non-viable elements in the cost of entry may occur in the production phase (i.e. cost of materials, plant and labour), in the market establishment phase (gaining an initial foothold in the market), or in the ongoing servicing phase (the cost of maintaining a leading position in that segment).

Exercise (Group):

Determine and discuss an industry in which 'cost of entry' would be a major consideration for an organisation considering a new market segment.

_____

_____

_____

_____

_____

_____

_____

_____

_____

_____

_____

_____

_____

_____

_____

_____

_____

_____

_____

_____

_____

Market Information

There are many different categories of information valuable to a company in segmenting its overall market and then selecting target markets from those segments. Similarly, there are many different sources of the various categories of information.

The research effort to acquire that information, as well as the information itself, is divided into two types — **primary** and **secondary**.

Primary information is that which is commissioned and collected specifically for the purpose at hand, i.e. in this instance, the company's decision-making process regarding segmentation of its marketplace, and selection of its target markets.

Secondary information is that which already exists and is usually held by external sources, having been commissioned or compiled for other purposes, general or specific.

Depending upon the category of information and specific purpose for which the organisation requires it, it might need to commission its own research (primary information) or, alternatively, secondary information (existing data from its own or external sources) might suffice.

It might even be more comprehensive and authoritative than commissioning its own research in this area. For example, commissioning certain types of research — such as that available from national census data — would be uneconomic and unnecessary.

Within these two types of information are another two types of information i.e. **qualitative** and **quantitative**.

Qualitative information is of a more subjective nature, i.e. opinion studies, behavioural research and other attitudinal data.	**Quantitative information** is that which deals predominantly with figures and quantifiable trends, such as geographic-based information obtained from census data.

Information Requirements

The different categories of market-related information likely to be required by an organisation in the process of segmenting its overall marketplace and selecting target markets, include (but are not limited to):

♦ *geographic statistics* with regard to potential segments;

♦ *demographic statistics* with regard to potential segments;

♦ *existing purchase pattern data* with regard to potential segments;

♦ *lifestyle research* with regard to potential segments;

♦ *attitudinal data* both with regard to the overall marketplace and the potential market segment;

♦ any data which will help the organisation determine the degree to which the *potential market segment* may perceive its need to be already met, to what degree, and by what product or substitute product;

♦ *competitive intelligence* (which includes the study of competitors' activities and strategies), both with regard to potential segments and to the existing overall marketplace;

- *societal trend analysis* with regard to the existing overall marketplace;

- relevant *political information* (possibly);

- relevant *environment information* (possibly).

Primary Information Sources

Sources of primary information pertaining to these data needs include (but are not limited to):

- questionnaires (e.g. shopping centre research);

- panel research or 'focus' groups (where a small group representing the potential market segment is brought together in an intensive interview situation to learn about the members' buying motivations);

- retail audits (to determine market shares of existing brands);

- attitude surveys (of representatives of the market segment in question);

- specialised research (designed to obtain either quantitative or qualitative data on any of a number of potential segmentation criteria);

- experiments or market testing on existing segments.

Secondary Information Sources

Sources of secondary information pertaining to these data needs include (but are not limited to):

♦ Australian Bureau of Statistics publications (the ABS has a wide range of publications extrapolating the data obtained from the latest Australian census, from an equally wide range of perspectives most of which are highly relevant to consumer marketers). The census data itself can be purchased on CD;

♦ specialist research companies produce their own offerings based on extrapolations and combinations of the census data. Like the ABS publications, these are useful for organisations segmenting their markets on geographic and demographic bases;

♦ specific research periodicals and other publications by major research houses like A.C. Nielsen and Roy Morgan Research;

♦ daily or business media (for coverage of specific issues, or specific issue coverage within a specific timeframe, organisations can commission or retain the services of a media monitoring agency);

♦ universities and other higher education institutions;

♦ market studies by advertising agencies;

♦ competitors' annual reports;

♦ existing customers, suppliers and distributors (information to be derived from these sources is usually in the realm of competitor intelligence);

♦ existing market and customer data and the various departments within the organisation itself;

♦ Government departments;

- Chambers of Commerce;

- business advisory services, including regional development authorities;

- industry and professional associations;

- industry peers;

- trade press (national and international);

- media representatives (again, the information derived from this source is usually in the realm of competitor intelligence, if the information has not already been reported);

- industry directories;

- libraries and librarians;

- specialist industry analysts (e.g. the Gartner Group);

- the Internet (e.g. competitors' websites; also, the large research houses and management consultancies carrying out publicly-available research often publicise their offerings on their websites);

- embassies, high commissions and consulates (in the case of international market and competitor intelligence);

- studies by the large accountancy and management consultancy firms (often particularly relevant to business-to-business, business-to-Government and industrial marketing);

- the Australian and New Zealand Standard Industrial Classification (ANZSIC) system is a valuable source of information for business-to-business marketers segmenting their marketplace by industry and company type.

In addition, the above sources of information can be combined - primary with primary, secondary with secondary, and primary with secondary - to provide greater depth of data and a more comprehensive and authoritative insight into the marketplace.

Exercise (Group):

Invent a consumer product organisation about to undertake segmentation of the market for a new product it is contemplating manufacturing (invent the product also). List the primary and the secondary sources of information the organisation might most valuably tap into to provide it with an authoritative picture of its marketplace. Also list the type or types of information likely to be obtained from each source.

_____

_____

_____

_____

_____

_____

_____

_____

_____

_____

_____

_____

_____

_____

_____

The Segmentation Process

A market can be segmented using any — or a combination — of the following methods:

1)   Geographic

2)   Demographic

3)   Psychographic

4)   Behavioural

Using these factors (usually in combination), marketers can identify useful 'target' groups which qualify themselves according to the similarity of their needs and wants, relevant to the 'benefits package' offered by the organisation's product or service.

For organisations wanting to service the total marketplace, identifying such segments within the overall market can allow them to develop a '**brand strategy**', i.e. a range of brands, each appealing to a different segment. Thus it can achieve greater coverage and penetration of the market than if it tried to service all segments with one brand or one product.

28

Let's investigate the various factors within each segmentation method.

Geographic Variables

When segmenting geographically, a market segment is identified using any or all of the following variables:

- country

- state / region

- city / population

- population density

- climate

- regional attitudes, preferences and parochialisms (sometimes)

Demographic Variables

Demographic segmentation variables include:

- age group

- gender

- income or wealth status

- social class

- nationality

- marital status

- family size and life stage

- education level

- occupation category

- religious beliefs

Psychographic Variables

Variables to be considered when segmenting a market upon its psychographics, include:

- lifestyle

- values

- personality

- influences

- shopping habits.

Behavioural Variables

Variables used in behavioural segmentation include:

- actual needs

- benefits sought

- purchase occasion

- frequency of purchase / use

- user status

- loyalty status

- product and purchase attitude

- brand attitude

- degree of convincing required

Now let's discuss each segmentation method and its variables.

Geographic Segmentation

Why would a company use geographic variables to segment its marketplace?

Where we live and work often dictates the nature of the various needs in our lives. For example, in large cities where people commute long distances, often arriving home late at night, there is greater demand for convenience stores and extended supermarket hours, pre-packaged meals, household services and so on.

Population density, of course, also plays a strong factor in the viability of servicing a geographic market.

Climate clearly has a dramatic affect on purchase and usage rates of many categories of products and services.

And regional attitudes and parochialisms can dictate strong preferences or otherwise for certain types of products, or brands with certain characteristics or images within different product categories.

Geographic segmentation not only helps determine basic viability for entering a market, but can also highlight the need for a specific and distinct marketing mix within any given country, state, region, or even city.

Here is a market segment identified via a typical geographic breakdown:

World Region: Asia-Pacific

Country: Australia

State: New South Wales

	City / City Area:	Greater Metropolitan Sydney
	City Status:	Urban with several concentrated business hubs in addition to the CBD, and significant and increasing suburban sprawl
	City Size:	4.1 Million
	Climate:	Temperate

Meantime, here are some sample category breakdown options for geographic segmentation:

State	Region	Population	City/Region Status	Climate
New South Wales Australian Capital Territory Victoria Queensland Western Australia South Australia Tasmania	Greater Metropolitan Sydney Victorian regional Queensland Gold Coast Western Australian country	Under 5000 5–19,999 20,000–49,999 50,000–99,999 100,000–49,999 500,000–999,999 1,000,000–4,999,999 5,000,000+	concentrated urban decentralised urban urban with suburban sprawl suburban regional town semi rural rural	hot dry hot/dry humid humid/heavy rainfall temperate cold heavy rainfall cold/heavy rainfall

Clearly, such factors dictate the market viability for all manner of products and services, from different food and beverage types, to home appliance types, to household services.

For example, a tinned soup manufacturer could conceivably find a greater market in a colder area, whilst an appliances manufacturer can readily predict greater potential for the sale of air conditioners in a hot, dry area than in a cold/heavy rainfall region.

However, there are many other factors at play in the marketplace, and next we will look at a market's demographic variables.

Demographic Segmentation

Demographic segmentation is the most common method used in determining a market. It often serves as the primary, or essential, base upon which other segmentation methods are layered.

Key demographic factors like age, gender, nationality and income are often principal determinants in the demand for a product or service.

For example, it could be reasonably assumed (and the assumption easily tested) that 10 to 15 year old males would present a more likely market opportunity for the new breed of foot scooter than 50-plus females.

Likewise, it is likely that professionally-employed, single, 'Anglo-Saxons' will be readier buyers of single-serve frozen gourmet meals than household heads of large families of European extraction.

Let's take a look at three of the major guiding variables in demographic segmentation:

Age group

Age is one of the most basic determinants in demographic segmentation. Clearly, our needs and wants evolve as we progress through the different age groups.

Different age groups can present significantly differing market potential for many products and services, and product decisions. Market entry decisions and marketing mix decisions often have this variable at their core.

Certain age groups represent very significant markets per se, based on factors like culture and societal trends.

Examples of this phenomenon include the large, trend-conscious teen market, and the ever-evolving baby boomers, the bulk of whom are currently in their middle years, with the front end of the boom heading past the 50 mark.

This particular group has been, demonstrably, one of the largest-spending, market-changing consumer groups in history.

Baby boomers have driven many of the world's largest consumer market trends, beginning with processed baby foods, moving through Barbie dolls and Matchbox toys, fast food, real estate, 'people mover' wagons and now creating new growth in sectors like financial or superannuation products, health insurance, personal care and travel.

Meantime, the baby boomers' children (falling in large proportion into what marketers have dubbed 'Generation Y') look set also to be a formidable force in dictating consumer trends and demand.

 However, 'Generation Y' — in its current predominantly teenage phase — represents a rapidly moving target for marketers. It is also a highly fragmented market. Take clothing fashions. Where, for example, its baby boomer parents were driving demand for a certain fashion or style of garment, Generation Y segments itself markedly, different segments declaring allegiance to different high-profile brands. Their selection is dependent upon which brand and style best expresses that group's values or the personality its members desire to project (usually to their peers).

And here we see the variables of psychographic segmentation coming into play, overlaid on the base demographic variable of age.

Consumer product organisations also make product line extension decisions on the variable of age. For example, USANA is a multi-level marketing company specialising in vitamins, related nutritional products and other personal care lines. One of its core products is its 'Essentials' antioxidant and multi-vitamin twin set.

Discovering that its adult market wanted its children to take nutritional supplements, but that youngsters, in general, found the 'adult size' tablets difficult to swallow, USANA launched a kids' 'Chewable' version of its Essentials product.

Gender

Some of the most interesting and controversial trends in consumer marketing have arisen from the gender role shifts of the past two decades.

Consider the imagery now used in many financial services, car and sportswear advertisements. There is an increasing representation of women — usually well-heeled, well-educated and independent women — in these sectors' advertising.

Toyota, for example, has run advertising campaigns for its Celica in magazines catering for the younger, self-supporting woman.

Meantime, a large financial sector player recently ran a Buspak advertising campaign depicting a young professional female who 'used to want to marry a millionaire', but now wants 'to be one'. And the portrayal of female athletes, or athletic female images, in sportswear and sports shoe advertising is now commonplace.

Similarly, while some products and services are predominantly purchased by one gender within a couple or family unit, the actual purchase decision might well be predominantly influenced by the other partner or another family member of the opposite gender.

Consider here the decision-making and purchasing processes associated with cars as one example, and home or garden maintenance services as another.

Gender considerations might provide organisations with the potential for growth through product line extensions. Analysis of the gender demographics of a market also provides the basis for dual-branding decisions within ranges of products like personal care items.

For example, a toiletries manufacturer might decide to introduce a female version of one of its lines, e.g. Tommy Hilfiger's 'Tommy Girl' fragrance as an example of successful product line extension based on gender demographics.

And, of course, some organisations' products and services are designed for and targeted specifically at one gender or the other.

In summary, the two genders can offer markets for different products and services, or differing markets for products and services, or represent different roles in the decision-making and purchase activity for different products and services, or represent market growth opportunities.

Evolving societal trends can also impact this particular demographic variable in significant ways over time.

Income or Wealth Status

Simply, this variable is all about consumer spending power. Not necessarily the preparedness to spend, but at least the capacity.

Clearly, there would be little point in a luxury car manufacturer selecting as a target market segment, say, families of blue collar workers with an average annual household income of less than $25,000.

Likewise, it would not be a strategic marketing decision for, say, marketers of an exclusive clothing label to pursue K Mart as part of their distribution strategy.

Snobbery can have very pragmatic elements in the budgetary environment of the marketing mix decision-making process.

A typical breakdown of the income variable for the purposes of segmentation might look like this:

Income:
Under $24,999
$25,000-$39,999
$40,000-$64,999
$65,000-$89,999
$90,000+

While some companies target the affluent and those in higher income brackets, the marketing strategies of others might very deliberately, and profitably, target lower-income earners.

It is important to realise that within this variable are 'subvariables' which make it unwise for some companies to take the issue of income at face value.

For example, many retirees are low-income earners yet, with their mortgages paid off and the nest long emptied of offspring, they might have a relatively high capacity for discretional spending.

It must be remembered though that income or wealth status is only an indication of the capacity to spend. The willingness to spend, and to spend on the product or service in question, is another issue. Here again, we see other variables like psychographic and behavioural, converging with a demographic factor.

Psychographic Segmentation

Psychographic variables are stronger indicators of people's 'emotional buying factors', than are geographic and demographic variables. Whilst geographic and demographic factors indicate the basic size and scope of a market, it is often psychographic factors (and behavioural factors, which we will discuss next) that play the role of the catalyst in the conversion of a prospect within a market segment into an actual customer.

Psychographic segments are less easily locatable and less easily measurable than geographic or demographically identified segments. However, as the general marketplace becomes flooded with choice and most products satisfy basic functional needs, marketers are increasingly using psychographic variables both to identify new market segments and increase existing ones, as well as to differentiate their offerings for competitive positioning.

Cars, today's teen clothing brands, higher-value cosmetic and personal care lines, travel and holiday destinations are all prime examples of products whose marketers rely heavily on psychographic variables for market segmentation and for points of differentiation in their marketing mixes.

Let's investigate three of the most common variables used in segmenting a market psychographically:

Lifestyle

Consumers express themselves, their opinions, beliefs and preferences through the products and services they buy and consume. Their lifestyle — how they live and how and with whom they spend their time — is also directly reflected in the products they buy and their brand choices.

For instance, would a single outdoor-sports loving executive who skies regularly and lives a highly-mobile, independent, hardworking and party-going lifestyle, in general terms, be representative of the market for a 'people-mover' vehicle like a Mitsubishi Starwagon or Toyota Tarago? What about a Honda CRX?

Lifestyle segmentation and positioning provides for great creativity in the image creation, 'packaging' and promotional phases of the marketing effort.

Personality

Personality represents another fertile field for a company seeking differentiating factors for its brand image.

Useful personality types for marketers of particular products and services might be, for example, 'freedom-loving', 'independent', 'individualistic', 'rebellious', 'security-conscious', 'responsible', 'leader', 'sensual', 'expressive', and so on.

Marketers can find profitable marketing opportunities by aggregating these personality types within market segments, as well as identify profitable differentiating or competitive positions, and build brand images with these 'personalities'.

Perfume is an ideal example of a product around which a distinct personality can be created, and which can, in turn, be marketed to that personality type. There are, of course, many examples of the positioning of such fragrances in the marketplace. Many are aligned with celebrities and other famous personalities.

However, it should be remembered that it is not as easy to locate and group personality types within a market as it is other more tangible variables like geographic and demographic factors.

Values

There is a close intersection of lifestyle and personality with values.

Values, however, dictate our deeper and subconscious needs. They drive us at a more fundamental level. They are a more inward reflection of who we are. They represent, in effect, our 'programming'.

Viewed in this light, and for the important conscious and subconscious motivators that they are in our lives, as a psychographic variable, values represent a very useful predictor of buying behaviour.

Behavioural Segmentation

Not to be confused with psychographic variables like personality, **behavioural segmentation** variables relate to a prospective customer's need/perceived need for, attitude towards, and usage of, the product or service being marketed.

Let's look at a range of behavioural variables.

Actual needs

Actual needs are the functional or fundamental, tangible, needs a consumer has of the product or service in question. A car buyer, first and foremost, requires transport. Someone purchasing toothpaste, above all else, requires a product that will clean his or her teeth. Someone buying washing powder wants his or her clothes to come out of the washing machine clean.

Benefits sought

Benefits sought can represent a far greater range of expectations of, or hopes for, a product's performance, or a service's impact, than simply those recognised as actual needs.

It is in this area that emotional buying needs come strongly into play, as do personal idiosyncrasies. For example, the car buyer may require peer recognition, the toothpaste buyer may want fewer trips to the dentist for her children, and the washing powder shopper may want the personal confidence he derives from sporting crisp, white shirts in the office.

Purchase occasion

This can refer to special occasions as recognised by society, the specific community, the family or the individual himself or herself. An example would be Easter, when confectionery companies enjoy their annual financial harvest.

Purchase occasion can also refer to time of day. For example, a bread manufacturer may promote its multi-grain loaf as the ideal lunchtime sandwich loaf.

Frequency of purchase / use

Frequency of purchase/use refers to the potential customer's level of awareness and experience of the brand, as well as his or her current rate of consumption of that product type.

Market segments for some products — particularly commodity products like many grocery items — can be easily identified for their light/occasional use, medium/reasonably regular use, or heavy/frequent use of a product.

To the extent that it is possible, marketers might also assess whether:

(a)   there is an existing level of awareness of the brand being marketed, to build on;

(b)   whether that awareness and prior exposure is favourable, and

(c)   what usage rate similarly positioned brands, if there are any, experience.

Degree of convincing required

This variable is a (subjective) measure of how much effort and investment in the marketing mix — particularly the promotional part — it will take to push the prospective buyer over the line and win his or her custom.

Some market segments, and certainly some products, require the provision of more pre-purchase information and promotional activity than do others.

42

Convergence of Variables

Attempting to segment a market based on one set of variables only (i.e. geographic, demographic, psychographic or behavioural) is usually of limited use to marketers.

However, combining different segmentation methodologies helps provide a clear and comprehensive picture of an organisation's potential markets, how to reach them and what marketing messages will appeal to those groups, as well as their true size and dollar value.

For instance, identifying a market segment as '25 to 35-year-old female professionals' (demographic), tells the marketer little about where that market is to be found (geographic), its buying motivations (behavioural), or what it is about the product or service that its members might relate to in an emotional sense.

Similarly, identifying a market segment as 'enjoys an independent lifestyle and outward self-expression' (psychographic), tells the marketer little about the whereabouts of this potential market (geographic), their capacity to buy the product or service in question (demographic), nor about the specific catalysts for their likely purchase of the product or service at any given point in time (behavioural).

Therefore, the most valuable approach to the use of the four categories of variables is a multi-variant approach, in which the different types of segmentation methodologies most relevant to the product or service being marketed are merged.

Much of marketing theory — and common logic — suggests the starting point for segmenting a market is to determine potential customers' reasons for buying the product or service.

The segmentation process, according to this philosophy, would then move forward to overlay these with the many and varied considerations of the other three segmentation methodologies.

Some marketers use computer programs to assist in this process. One of the most common computer-assisted segmentation practices is the '**cluster analysis**'.

In the cluster analysis, data from identified geographic and demographic segments is merged with data of a psychographic and behavioural nature, to 'cluster' customers together in groups according to similarities in these chosen variables.

This is based on the theory that, having strategically selected the variables to use as a basis for identifying these clusters, the potential customers falling into each will respond in a similar manner to a certain market positioning and marketing mix with regard to the product or service being marketed.

Segment Descriptors Used in Consumer Marketing

Whether judgment-based or computer assisted, this further refining stage in the segmentation process calls in the need for names to be given to each 'cluster' or market segment representing the combination of selected marketing variables.

Usually organisations and their marketing departments or market research agencies invent their own catchy and self-descriptive names for these market segments.

Let's take the marketplace for cable television as a hypothetical example.

Our imaginary cable TV marketer might use geographic, demographic and psychographic segmentation to determine its ultimate target markets.

In doing so, it comes up with the following four major market segments, which it dubs:

1)   Recliners
2)   Boom Box Babes
3)   Metros
4)   Must Haves

The first group, 'Recliners', demonstrates the following characteristics: low to moderate income, values leisure time, outer suburb dwellers.

Meantime, the relevant characteristics demonstrated by the 'Boom Box Babes' group are: under 25, peer pressure driven, working-middle class suburb dwellers.

The next group, the 'Metros', demonstrates these characteristics: moderate to high income, current affairs conscious, inner city suburb dwellers.

The fourth group, the 'Must Haves', demonstrates these characteristics: high income, consumerists, middle-upper class suburb dwellers.

Thus, both converging the various segmentation methodologies and giving self-descriptive names to the resultant segments, produces a more comprehensive and commercially useful picture of the available market segments, as well as providing a clearer insight into the market positioning and marketing mix which is likely to appeal to each.

Exercise (Group):

Determine the most relevant segmentation methodologies for:

- ◆ bathroom soap

_____

_____

_____

- ◆ yoghurt

_____

_____

_____

- ◆ imported beer

_____

_____

_____

- ◆ just-add-sauce fresh pasta dinners

_____

_____

_____

Additional Segmentation Considerations for Service Markets

With service industries becoming more competitive and, at the same time, more marketing-oriented, other bases for segmentation are emerging in this sector.

In addition to the variables that apply in the consumer product market, service firms are employing considerations like current and future profitability (to the service-provider), likelihood of increasing the firm's share of related services provision and, where the prospective client is not a consumer of the firm's other services, how likely that 'prospect' is to leave their current service provider in favour of the firm in question.

Segmenting Industrial or Business-to-Business Markets

Business or industrial markets are segmented for precisely the same reason as are consumer — or end-user — markets. That is, grouping prospective customers into, for example, representations of the same needs, buying motivations and capacities, and geographic factors, makes for a more proficient and cost-effective marketing effort.

One of the obvious starting points for segmenting an industrial or business market is by industry or sector. That is, an industrial or business-to-business marketer might first choose to view his or her market in terms of which of the following categories it falls into:

- Non-profit

- Multinational

- Large national

- Medium-sized enterprise

- Small business

Alternatively, depending upon its product or service, it might choose to start with a sector breakdown of its overall marketplace e.g.:

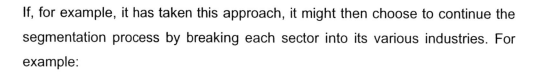

- Manufacturing

- Professional services

- Banking and finance

- Retail

If, for example, it has taken this approach, it might then choose to continue the segmentation process by breaking each sector into its various industries. For example:

> **Manufacturing**: Glass; food and beverages; furniture; pharmaceuticals and others.

Other segmentation variables, which could be used either as the primary factor, or in combination with other factors, include:

Customer / Client Location

Similarly to the consumer product market, industrial and business-to-business marketers need to ensure a particular market can be segmented viably and, for some companies, this either restricts, or at least dictates their focus on, certain geographic areas. This is particularly so in the case of companies with a significant service component to their offering, especially where that service is provided by the company's own employees.

This variable is similar to the geographic segmentation factors used for consumer product markets.

Demographics

Demographic segmentation also applies to industrial and business-to-business markets, but with a different set of variables. These include company size/ number of employees, number of locations, and sales volume.

Demographic variables in this type of market will also include factors that are relevant in some industries but not so important, as classifiers, in others. This includes length of time in operation, customer growth rate or share of its own marketplace.

Corporate Culture

'Corporate culture' in the industrial or business market is similar in its marketing implications to the psychographic and behavioural variables used in consumer marketplace segmentation.

For example, whether a company is 'young, innovative and aggressive', or whether it is 'staid and conservative', will impact upon the types of products and services it favours, the volumes it orders them in, and factors like how long it takes in the decision making process.

Quality, Service or Price Focus

This variable relates to the order of priority a customer/client organisation places on quality, service or price with regard to the product or service being marketed.

Some suppliers will be stronger on quality than service; some will be stronger on price competitiveness, and so on. Marketers should know their inherent competitive strengths and use this knowledge to segment their markets strategically.

Purchase and Usage

Marketers must also consider where purchase decisions are made both within the various geographic locations of a customer / client organisation, and within the power structure of the organisation itself. For example, given the particular product or service being marketed, it may be more strategic to go after companies with a concentration of buying power in their operations divisions, or their IT departments or, alternatively, their marketing departments.

Into this category of variable falls the decision of whether an organisation focuses on customers or clients with whom it is already doing business, or whether it is best served by trying to attract new clientele.

Other purchase and usage variables include:

- Known purchasing preferences, e.g. tenders and sealed bids, leasing, negotiated outright purchase;

- Order volumes, i.e. does the segment represent potentially large orders?

- Product usage, i.e. a product marketer might decide to focus on one specific type of use for its product or, alternatively, on a broad range of uses for its product. This will help determine the relevant market segments.

Supplier Relationship Norms

Marketers must ask the question, does this segment have long-standing supplier relationships that would be hard to break?

This consideration will help marketers determine whether or not it is worthwhile making the investment to cater for and cultivate companies with other existing allegiances, or with particular expectations with regard to supplier relationships and performance, in the area of their specific product or service.

Exercise (Group):

Discuss prominent examples of industrial or business-to-business marketers (product or service), and determine broadly the variables each appears to use in segmenting its markets.

_____

_____

_____

_____

_____

_____

_____

_____

_____

_____

_____

_____

_____

_____

_____

_____

_____

_____

_____

Audiences within Market Segments

Within any given market segment is a range of 'audiences', each of whom play a different role in the purchase decision and consumption of the product or service. These include:

- Influencers

- Decision makers

- Purchasers

- Ultimate consumers

Take the consumer product-marketing example of a brand of frozen TV dinner. A key influencer might be the pre-school age child accompanying the mother in the supermarket. The decision maker will be (one hopes) the mother; the purchaser also the mother; and the ultimate consumers will be the mother, the father, the pre-school child and its school-age siblings.

On a micro level, beginning the marketing process with careful market segmentation, strategic selection of target markets and a detailed profiling of each target market, provides a clear picture of each group within the selected market segment.

It also provides direction for the organisation in its research into the marketing considerations dictated by each such group within the target market.

On a macro level, the greater the understanding of the motivation of each participant involved in or influencing purchase and consumption, along with the dynamics at play, the more accurate the foundation upon which to base the overall marketing strategy.

Exercise (Group):

Select a product or service. Discuss the importance of a detailed understanding of the various subgroups involved in the purchase decision and ultimate consumption of that product or service.

Your Challenges (Individual):

1. Select an organisation involved in more than one type of marketplace or marketplace strata. Provide your written views on the various subgroups involved in the purchase decision for its product or service within each of its markets.

2. Taking the hypothetical example of a large stationery and office supplies chain, determine the most strategic variables it might use to segment its overall marketplace. Then identify the different audiences within the likely segments, and who (in terms of job role) might represent the influencers, the decision makers, the purchasers and the ultimate consumers.

_____

_____

_____

_____

_____

_____

_____

_____

_____

_____

_____

_____

_____

Reviewing the Segmentation Process

If the market segmentation process has been conducted correctly, the various segments will have emerged via the identification of broad groups with needs relevant to the product or service and its benefits.

The process will then have moved back through a narrowing down stage, whereby the large, all-encompassing market was divided into smaller groups. These potential customers will have been grouped together on the basis of the members of each having similar needs and buying motivations.

Each segment will, therefore, as a differentiated market segment, be as distinct as possible from all other identified segments, in terms of its needs relevant to the product or service in question.

Reviewing further, these preliminary identified segments will then have been further shaped by geographic, demographic, psychographic and behavioural variables.

Now the marketer must identify the most strategic of those identified market segments, as a target market or markets.

An Important Reminder About Segments

Remember, in arriving at your breakdown of segments from which to select the actual target market, you will have ensured that each of the segments is:

♦ Measurable	♦ Identifiable	♦ Accessible
♦ Substantial	♦ Distinguishable	♦ 'Homogenous'
♦ Stable	♦ Practical to service (profitably)	

Section 4:
Identifying Your Target Market

Target Market Strategy Options

There are four basic target market selection strategies available to marketers:

1)   Mass marketing

2)   Single segment

3)   Multiple segment

4)   Niche marketing

Mass Marketing

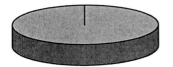

The **mass marketing** strategy is also known as *'undifferentiated'* marketing.

As the name suggests, this strategy involves grouping all segments of the organisation's marketplace together, and treating the market as one, undifferentiated mass.

Most large consumer product corporations and larger service-based organisations serving the consumer market, moved away from mass marketing decades ago. As the consumer environment evolved, increased production levels, competition from a greater number of brands and increased consumer choice, forced companies to leave behind their production-oriented approach to business and adopt a marketing approach.

This provided the foundation for today's more sophisticated marketing practices, particularly the concept of target marketing.

However, there are both reasons for, and instances in which, organisations would decide on a mass market strategy.

These include:

- Where consumers — viewed as an overall group — demonstrate a similar nature of demand and buying motivations for the product or service.

- In line with the above, where most consumers of the product or service view its benefits reasonably generically.

- Where the product is very much a commodity in nature e.g. baking soda.

- Instances in which a single marketing program will appeal to, and service the majority of, consumers.

The **benefits** of a mass marketing approach include:

1)   Limited Brand and Product Development Costs

With a singular approach to the overall marketplace, a company need produce only the one brand and/or product type. Thus, research and development costs, and any other investment or expense associated with getting the product to the production stage, is reduced.

2)   Rationalised Production Costs

If, for example, a manufacturing organisation has only to tool up for one brand and version of its product, clearly its production costs are greatly minimised compared with the company producing multiple brands and product versions, which must tool up and run a production line for each. This includes key components like packaging.

Similarly, a service organisation has only to develop one version of its service, limiting its expenses in this area to the one set of skills required for development and delivery of that singular service.

3)   *Rationalised Inventory Costs*

Again in the specific case of manufacturing organisations, inventory costs are limited to those involved in carrying stocks of the single brand or product type.

4)   *Rationalised Distribution Costs*

A singular marketing mix means a singular distribution strategy and rationalised transport costs.

5)   *Rationalised Cost of Promotion*

With only one set of advertisements, one set of printed promotional componentry, one strategy for promotional campaigns and only one marketing support strategy to focus on, the company's promotion-related expenses are both reduced and at the same time concentrated.

An organisation deciding on a mass marketing strategy would typically endeavour to gain a competitive advantage for its singular brand or product through '*product differentiation*'.

This involves a positioning strategy whereby the organisation's marketers use the various elements of the marketing communications mix (which might also include packaging) to highlight a selected aspect of the product or service which, it hopes, will 'position' it as superior in the collective mind of the marketplace. (Note: 'Positioning' will be covered in the next chapter.)

Consider the case of the Duracell bunny - the irresistible, battery-operated, drum-playing rabbit.

In the ultimate commodity product scenario, the battery market, Duracell created a superior image for its product with its savvy, bunny-supported positioning statement, that 'Duracell Batteries Keep on Keeping On'.

There are, of course, many **limitations** and **disadvantages** for the organisation deciding on a mass marketing strategy.

Amongst these are:

1) Competition

Almost every supplier to both the overall market for an organisation's product or service, as well as suppliers in every segment of that overall marketplace, becomes its competition. If the company is entering a new market, or an existing market with a new product, it will have to work harder for its share of that market, than had it selected only one segment, or a limited number of segments.

2) Customer Satisfaction Levels

The organisation with only one brand or product type and marketing mix cannot, in general, hope to service its customers as well as its target or niche market focused competitors. Therefore, the mass marketer will always sacrifice a certain proportion of market share to other suppliers more closely identifying and servicing the needs of specific segments within the overall market.

3) Less Substantial Product Differentiation

The mass marketing organisation has to work harder to find a substantial point of difference for its product, in order to develop a competitive position for it within the marketplace. When it does decide on a point of difference, it then must ensure it is likely to be a meaningful one for all segments of the overall market.

4)   Reduced Profit Potential

Maximising competition minimises profit potential. In many product scenarios, the market will naturally evolve into segments distinguishable by their levels of profitability. As a natural course of marketing events, the various competitor organisations will begin to concentrate their efforts on these more profitable segments of the originally undifferentiated marketplace, bringing about an inevitable targeting of these opportunity sectors.

Exercise (Group):

Identify a consumer product organisation successfully taking the mass-market approach. Discuss the possible reasons it pursues mass marketing.

_____

_____

_____

_____

_____

_____

_____

_____

_____

_____

_____

_____

_____

_____

_____

_____

_____

Single-Segment Marketing

When viewed from a market perspective, this target
market selection strategy is termed 'single-segment
marketing'. When viewed from a product perspective,
it is sometimes termed 'concentrated marketing'.

Single-segment marketing involves the selection of only one specific segment
from all the potentially targetable segments that have been identified.

An organisation wishing to hold a large share of a smaller part of the overall
market would adopt this strategy. It would also be the strategy selected by a
company wishing to be seen as specialist, either in servicing a particular
segment of the market, or in the manufacture / provision of a certain type /
image of service or product.

There are many reasons an organisation's marketers would decide to pursue a
single-segment — or concentrated — marketing strategy.

These include:

1)   'Specialist' Positioning

Concentrating on — and limiting its presence to — a single market segment
provides an organisation with the opportunity to attribute 'specialist' status to its
brand, giving it 'premium' positioning within the chosen segment.

If an organisation is successful with this positioning, it can achieve brand
leadership within that segment.

Bose stereo speakers provide an example of the 'premium' positioning a brand can enjoy when it produces a high-quality product and focuses on a single segment of the market. Bose focuses on sound quality connoisseurs with a high level of disposable income.

Another example of this marketing strategy employed at the other end of the socio-economic scale is 'K Mart'. While customers from all walks of life may actually shop at K Mart, it goes squarely after the value-oriented and budget-conscious shopper.

As a result of this target market selection strategy it might not enjoy the huge profit margins associated with many premium brands, but it enjoys the volume-related profitability resulting from being a standard port of call for its specific, but nonetheless substantial, chosen segment.

2)   Rationalised Costs

This might or might not be of primary concern to the marketer but, nonetheless, as with mass marketing, the cost of appealing to and servicing the needs of only a specific market segment represents significant cost savings over a multiple segment approach.

Costs are rationalised across the board, from development, production, inventory, warehousing, distribution and transport, through to every element of the marketing communications mix.

It makes good sense for an organisation with limited resources to adopt a single-segment marketing strategy, whereby those resources are concentrated on its chosen segment, as opposed to spread insufficiently across the broader market, or a number of different segments, where better-resourced companies are stronger players.

3)   Superior Ability

To become a force — or even a long-term player — in a market segment, a company must possess superior ability to satisfy the needs of that segment.

Thus, if an organisation identifies a segment it is able to service in a superior manner to its competitors, it makes good sense to concentrate on it.

However, there are **limitations** involved in selecting the single-segment target marketing strategy. Amongst these are:

1)   Reliance

A company that has placed itself in a position of reliance upon one market segment is in a vulnerable position.

For example, an organisation identifying a market segment as holding high growth potential may develop that segment into a very profitable one, only to find that its success in doing so attracts the attention of larger players with the resources to enter and compete aggressively.

2)   Image

An organisation with long-range plans to enter other segments of the overall market should think carefully before potentially creating an indelible image for its brand as providing one very specific type or quality of product, or servicing one narrow market segment.

It might be difficult for an organisation to successfully take the entrenched characteristics of its brand image into another market segment. The marketplace in general may be unable to relate to that brand as one which sits comfortably in the new market segment.

Group Exercise:

Identify and discuss examples of high-profile single-segment focused companies.

_____

_____

_____

_____

_____

_____

_____

_____

_____

_____

_____

_____

_____

_____

_____

_____

_____

_____

_____

_____

_____

Multiple-Segment Marketing

Marketers adopting a multiple-segment approach select two or more specific segments to enter. These it treats as different markets and services them with different brands, and/or different versions of its core product or service, and develops a different positioning and marketing program for each.

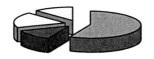

A typical example in the FMCG (Fast-Moving Consumer Goods) arena is breakfast cereal.

Uncle Toby's is a major force across the total breakfast cereal category. However, it holds its status by having achieved substantial shares in the various segments comprising the overall cereal market.

Uncle Toby's services the 'family' segment of its marketplace with its 'Oat Temptations' range of porridge products. It services the 'adult premium' segment of its market with its Flakes Plus range.

It also services the health-conscious segment with its Healthwise range of specialty cereals, each product within that range sporting a name self-descriptive of further segmentation within that broader health-conscious segment i.e. Healthwise Bowel, Healthwise for Your Heart, and Healthwise for Women 40-Plus.

Finally, having established its foothold across the category, Uncle Toby's extended its presence in the grocery sector by entering the oat-based snack food market with muesli bars and the Break Free range of oven-baked bars and cookies.

In this example, the manufacturer has developed different products to penetrate the various segments of the overall market. However, differentiation (as this target market selection strategy is also referred to) can also be achieved more simply. It can position its product differently in each market segment, for example, highlighting different uses or benefits in each.

The **benefits** available to an organisation opting for a multiple-segment approach to its marketing include:

1)   Market Coverage

A multiple-segment marketing organisation achieves greater coverage within the overall marketplace. This has obvious implications for sales volumes.

If an organisation can amortise its costs of production over multiple market segments, it increases the margin between total production cost and the increased sales volume it will enjoy from its presence in those segments.

2)   Brand Dominance

Brand dominance is a key goal for companies choosing a multiple-segment marketing strategy.

If a brand has a presence in all segments of the market, then it has a relevance to, and potential place in the lives of, the marketplace per se.

Brand dominance and market leadership go hand-in-hand. There are many reasons an organisation would pursue this strategy. For example, a brand enjoying dominance in the overall marketplace will enjoy, by default, a significant proportion of that marketplace, e.g. 'safe buy' perception.

3)   Adaptable Brand Image

A brand with a significant presence across different segments of the market has a greater likelihood of acceptance when it enters a new market segment.

For example, when Uncle Toby's introduced its muesli bars to the grocery sector's snack food category, consumers were well-used to seeing the various high-profile breakfast cereal products carrying the brand. Therefore, it wasn't a large transition to make from the cereal shelves, to the snack food shelves, with its oat-based muesli bars.

However, K Mart-branded boutiques selling international designer labels would have a hard time establishing market credibility.

There are, of course, **disadvantages** to the multiple-segment marketing strategy. These include:

1)   Cost Multiplication

Multiple brands or multiple versions of a product mean multiplied development, production, inventory, distribution and promotional costs.

2)   Spread of Focus

In very large corporates where a brand or product manager would manage each brand, product or market segment individually, this may not pose a problem. However, for organisations able to afford entry to a variety of market segments but for whom such a dedicated staffing structure is not viable, there exists the risk of diffusion of focus with regard to staffing and other resources.

Another option for multiple-segment marketers is to combine their selected target segments into one and service this combination of segments with one marketing mix.

The advantages of this joint segmentation strategy would be the reduction of cost and a lesser spread of management resources. However, these would represent a trade-off against the ability to address the needs of each original segment to the same degree, and therefore possibly against achieving the same penetration as would a separate approach for each.

Group Exercise:

Identify a multiple-segment marketer which offers the same product to its various chosen segments, differentiating its offering in terms of the type of use it promotes to each segment (as opposed to offering a different product per segment).

_____
_____
_____
_____
_____
_____
_____
_____
_____
_____
_____
_____
_____
_____
_____
_____
_____
_____

Niche Marketing

Niche marketing could be described as a *'super-concentrated'* single-segment approach.

A '**niche**' is a small submarket, a market within a market, a market with very specialist needs.

The benefits and the disadvantages of niche marketing are similar to the single-segment strategy, except magnified.

For example, concentrating on a niche market requires potentially fewer resources than any other target market selection strategy. It also potentially offers the opportunity to 'own' that specific market space. Further, it offers the brand or product servicing the niche the opportunity to develop a 'specialist' image and potentially enjoy the premium pricing such a tag justifies. Further still, it offers marketers the opportunity to learn a significant amount about their customers, and allows greater ease of detecting emerging trends and other change factors within their niche segments.

On the other hand, a niche-marketing organisation places its reliance on one very narrow segment of the market and therefore is highly vulnerable to the potential entry of new competitors with deep corporate pockets who have recognised the attractiveness or the growth of that specialist segment.

Group Exercise:

Identify and discuss a niche marketer and its marketing strategy.

_____

_____

_____

_____

_____

_____

_____

_____

_____

_____

_____

_____

_____

_____

_____

_____

_____

_____

_____

Selecting the Target Market Strategy

Not to be confused with selecting the actual market segments themselves, selecting the appropriate target market involves a careful assessment of:

1) *The company's product or service type.*

A company with a product of a commodity nature, with little scope for differentiation, might be best to employ a mass marketing approach. At the other end of the scale, marketers of a high-end, exclusively priced imported sound system might be best to employ either a single-segment or a niche market approach.

2) *The company's production and marketing resources.*

An organisation with relatively few resources might sensibly opt for a niche or single-segment strategy. However, a well-resourced organisation might opt for brand dominance through the more comprehensive market coverage of a multiple-segment strategy.

3) *The sophistication of the marketplace with regard to the product or service in question.*

If the market for a product has matured, marketers will likely need to target their offering specifically, or offer a highly differentiated product, in order to avoid investing in a market with little growth potential.

Alternatively, if a product concept or category is new, marketers might choose to introduce it to a broader marketplace.

4)   The degree of competition within the marketplace and where it is concentrated.

If the market for a particular product or service is rife with competition, it might be strategic for a company to take either a niche market or a single-segment approach, where it can achieve superior competitive positioning for its offering.

5)   The company's long-range objectives.

Marketers whose primary objectives include, as an example, 'brand dominance and market leadership within the next five years', and who have the resources to support that objective, might most strategically embark upon a multiple-segment assault of the marketplace.

Group Exercise:

Compile a list of six hypothetical companies and their products, each with their own specific marketing-oriented considerations. Determine the best target marketing strategy for each. Discuss your decisions.

_____

_____

_____

_____

_____

_____

_____

_____

_____

_____

Selecting the Target Segment or Segments

In selecting the actual target segment or segments which will comprise its niche, single-segment or multiple-segment marketing approach (whichever of these strategies it has opted for), the organisation has general principles of selection, as well as criteria unique to its own circumstances, to consider.

Marketers might have any number of underlying strategies, criteria or considerations that, themselves, help direct the strategy selected for target market selection.

General criteria include, as an example, *profitability*.

Whilst that seems to be stating the obvious, marketers sometimes become incorrectly focused on the organisation's capacity to win share in a market segment, despite the absence of any significant level of profitability, either in the immediate, or longer, term.

Accessibility is another criterion that, in the case of all organisations, should be a general qualifier of a market segment. Like profitability, accessibility is a pre-requisite in the initial identification of segments.

Meantime, considerations specific to an organisation's product or service might, for example, include the issue of *price sensitivity* in certain product or service categories.

The organisation's product or service might be one which experiences considerable price sensitivity, as in the case of the commodity, baking soda. Such circumstances would potentially limit marketers' options with regard to the target market strategies available to it.

Other considerations or, alternatively, underlying strategies that would influence target market strategies include *sales volume* requirements, overall *market share* objectives, the organisation's *purchasing power*, and *ease of entry* into the marketplace or specific segments thereof.

Others might include the compatibility of the intended strategy with the organisation's *corporate or brand image*. And yet other unique considerations might include the organisation's own *corporate direction*. For example, it might be on an intended path of significant growth, which would dictate entry into segments which themselves offer some form of substantial growth potential.

Profiling the Selected Market Segments

When developing a specific customer profile, the members of a segment market are described according to their similarities in the variables of geography, demography, psychography and behaviour, relevant to the product or service being marketed. They may be additionally described using other market or product-relevant considerations.

Firstly, though, let's review the **primary categories of marketing variable**. The table on the next page outlines a range of key descriptors within each of the four types of variables. The information contained in the 'Specific Examples' column, therefore, profiles a hypothetical market segment formed by the convergence of all four segmentation methods.

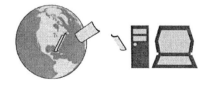

Primary Categories of Marketing Variables

Variables Set	Key Descriptors	Specific Examples
Geographic	Global region	Asia-Pacific
	Country	Australia
	State/region	South Australia
	City	Adelaide
	Population	1.5 million
	Population density	Urban/surburban
	Climate	Temperate/dry
Demographic	Age group	35-49
	Gender	Male
	Income	$65,000-$99,000
	Social class	Middle
	Nationality	'Anglo Saxon'
	Family size and life stage	Married, children under 10
	Education level	TAFE or university
	Occupation category	Professional, technical or management
	Religious beliefs	Catholic, Protestant, Methodist or Anglican
Psychographic	Lifestyle	Family, social
	Values	Security, sense of belonging, sense of achievement
	Personality	Ambitious but not risk-taking
	Influences	Professional and community peers
	Shopping attitude	Delegator
Behavioural	Benefits sought	Superior performance, durability, reliability
	Purchase occasion	Occasional and researched
	Frequency of purchase/use	Replacement, five-year average
	User status	Frequent
	Loyalty status/brand attitude	Moderate brand loyalty
	Product and purchase attitude	Measured, optimistic

Developing the Profile

Again, the information in the 'Specific Examples' column provides the basis of a specific consumer profile.

This information would typically be derived from, or supported by, in-depth consumer / market research, which would be detailed in a more comprehensive analysis of the market segment or consumer group.

Marketers can choose the form of consumer profiling that best meets their needs and is most relevant to their product or service.

As an example, a consumer profile summary based on the example in the table might read as follows:

> *35-49 year old professional Anglo-Saxon males with a medium level of disposal income; security-conscious with family values; and living in greater metropolitan Adelaide. A careful, moderately brand-loyal, regular user seeking performance, durability and reliability, and who may or may not be the actual purchaser of replacement product.*

Some marketers prefer values-led consumer profiles, for example:

> *Socially-aware, 'middle youth' consumers of moderate to above average means, balancing personal needs and desires with societal and environmental responsibility.*

Others prefer snappier segment descriptions, such as :

> *'Wealthy, Outer-directed Conspicuous Consumers.'*

© Jordan Kelly

Segment Descriptors

Some marketers develop catchphrases for their market segments e.g. *'Land Lubbers'* or *'Born to Wear'*.

The following table outlines a hypothetical example of a golf club employing a multiple-segment strategy to market memberships. The table shows the use of this form of catchphrase-based consumer profile. As you can see, the use of catchphrases as a naming practice for market segments helps draw the comparisons between each.

Multiple-Segment Strategy

Segment	Consumer Characteristics	Buying Motivators
Pros	Serious golfers, love the game, open age range, mostly professional or qualified tradespeople, predominantly male but increasing proportion of females	Quality of golf course, distance from home and ease of access, hours, range of benefits offered by membership package
Networkers	35 to 55 age bracket, male, senior and account management positions (especially in service-based corporations)	Proportion of business decision makers in membership base
Twilighters	Over 55, retired or semi-retired, recreational golfers, both genders	Cost, proportion of peers and friends in membership base
Toe Dippers	25 to 45, first-time golfers, mostly younger professionals, both genders	Cost, membership benefits offered in addition to basics

A 2002 study by international management consultancy Accenture, provides an actual, recent example of this practice.

The objective of the study was to update the understanding held by the Australian commercial sector at large, with regard to the effect technology is having on the media, entertainment and other habits of the Australian public.

Using the results of the study, Accenture divided the Australian community into five market segments: the early adopters whom they dubbed 'Switched-on Cybers' (15 percent), followed in their rate of technology adoption by 'Digital Absorbers' (38 percent), 'Tech Pragmatics' (20 percent), 'Techno Learners' (18 percent) and 'Digi-Nots' (9 percent).

(This is an example of market segmentation carried out on the primary basis of behavioural variables.)

A market segment or consumer profile is used as the basis for decisions ranging from product and service development, target market selection, level of investment in market entry, positioning, packaging and the marketing communications mix.

Your Challenge (Individual):

Outline a product concept and then identify a range of market segments its manufacturer might wish to enter.

1) Conduct this segmentation using geographic, demographic, psychographic and behavioural variables.

2) Give each market segment a name, based on the characteristics of the customer group it personifies.

3) Develop a specific consumer profile for the selected segment or segments.

4) Determine the optimum target market selection strategy and outline your logic.

5) Finally, provide a basic list of factors dictating the attractiveness or otherwise of each identified market segment.

_____

_____

_____

_____

_____

_____

_____

_____

_____

_____

_____

_____

_____

_____

_____

Section 5:
Developing a Positioning Strategy

What is 'Positioning' and why 'Position' A Service or Product?

Positioning is at the heart of marketing strategy.

This concept involves claiming a certain 'position' for the product or service both in the market and in the minds of its target consumers. Selecting the target market segments determines the base requirements of the positioning blueprint.

A smart company realises there is little choice but to determine and go after a specific marketplace and competitive position. Customers will form their own perceptions of the product if it doesn't. And so it uses the positioning opportunity to its advantage.

On the other hand, an organisation which fails to determine and successfully claim a strategic spot for its product or service in the market and consumer mindspace will find its position dictated for it, by the assumptions of consumers, by competitors, or by general market forces.

In most instances, the positioning attained by default will place the organisation at a competitive disadvantage.

A company that is not proactive in positioning might find its service or product holding a position amidst a nonviable degree of competition. Alternatively, it might find itself in an unprofitable or unattractive position because it failed to claim a more strategic spot through its marketing mix. Or it might simply find its product or service floating undifferentiated within the marketplace.

Strong and strategic market positioning are critical to fundamental marketing objectives like product profitability, growth, company and product image, brand credibility and market share.

The positioning of a brand / service / product within the marketplace, and the concept of 'differentiation' go hand-in-hand. An offering must first differentiate itself from competitors' brands / products / services. It then uses that point / those points of differentiation as its competitive strength.

A company can use the same principles as will be outlined in this chapter to 'reposition' an existing product or service. Repositioning can be a useful strategy when, for example, the product or service in question has attracted significant competition for its position since it first entered the market, or when a product or service — and demand for it — has reached maturity.

Unique Selling Proposition (USP)

A term often used for the 'position' resulting from the differentiation process is 'Unique Selling Proposition'.

Commonly abbreviated and referred to as the 'USP', the Unique Selling Proposition is the fundamental or chief difference in an organisation's offering over that of its competitors. Ideally, as the term suggests, the differentiating factor or factors must be sufficiently substantial as to create a genuine 'uniqueness' about the product or service.

The USP underpins the target marketing strategy and market segment selection logic.

USP is most commonly used to reflect the differentiated position of the product or service when that differentiation is based on tangible elements. However, it is possible for positioning to be attained by image factors alone, and we will investigate this shortly.

When an organisation selects a desired positioning based on superiority in any tangible factor, it must ensure its product performs to the promised standard or delivers the promised benefit.

Positioning based on the creation of an expectation, or set of expectations, in the minds of consumers, must be solid and real.

Opportunities for Differentiation

Differentiation can be achieved in a surprisingly large number of areas in most product categories. However, all are elements or extrapolations of either the product itself, or the service issues surrounding it.

Product

In terms of product, an organisation can choose from differentiating factors such as:

1) Quality

Superior quality is one of the most obvious competitive positioning choices. Whilst many companies unconvincingly flog the quality message in the absence of a more creative positioning strategy, others have built their entire reputations on it. Miele kitchen appliances represent a classic example.

2) Features

Think mortgage lenders as an example. The advertising campaigns of many such organisations position their home loans on certain features like 'no establishment fees'.

3) Benefits

Usually the result of certain actual features of the product or service, but promoted from the perspective of a benefit.

To use the mortgage market example again, a lender might position its loan as being structured for quicker payment completion. This is, in fact, the theme of one of Aussie Home Loans' recent advertising campaigns, with large billboards in key traffic corridors encouraging commuters to 'Get Home Sooner'.

4) Price

An organisation choosing to emphasise its pricing in its USP would more than likely be emphasising a low-price, or 'value' pricing. The market position of another product or service might, of course, involve a premium pricing structure, but it would be the way / ways in which the product or service is superior (e.g. a 'luxury' brand) that would be emphasised, not the high pricing itself.

5) Performance

Think cars as an example. BMW is positioned both as a status symbol and as the 'ultimate performance machine'.

6) Style

Certain home appliances and whitegoods manufacturers, for example, attempt a premium market positioning through use of stylish or distinctive design.

7) Environmental Friendliness

Brands like the 'Green Choice' range of household cleaning products project their company mission into the marketplace in a strong positioning statement. Green Choice product packaging, for example, features the World Wide Fund for Nature panda bear logo and a constant reminder that a proportion of profit from the sale of each product benefits that foundation and its efforts. (It also donates a portion of its products to OzGreen.)

An endless number of product-based differentiation strategies exist to support the chosen market positioning for a product or service.

Service

Similarly, there are many options available to the creative marketer for differentiating the service component of a product offering, or differentiating the service product per se.

These include:

1) Guarantees

Certain product manufacturers have developed market confidence in their product through their own belief in the unrivalled quality of their product, some going as far as to make 'lifetime guarantees' part of their offerings.

Most car manufacturers use this service component of an otherwise product offering to gain a competitive edge for their products. Most include a three-year (100,000-kilometre) warranty as part of the package. Some manufacturers try to secure an extra competitive edge by providing a five-year or 150,000-kilometre warranty. A smaller number of particularly adventurous vehicle manufacturers try to secure a greater competitive edge still, by taking the calculated risk of offering a five-year or unlimited kilometre warranty.

2) Technical Support

ISP (Internet Service Provider) accounts provide an example of a supporting service behind a service, and how that support service can become a powerful positioning strategy. ISPs who offer 24-hour 'help desks' and shorter phone queues to access them are an attractive option to many Internet users.

3) Standards of Service

The international Dominoes Pizza empire originally built its positioning statement on speed of service, based on its self-challenge of pizza delivery within a certain number of minutes.

3) Convenience

In this Internet age, Australia's own *greengrocer.com.au* success story came into being by identifying a new convenience-based concept in fruit and vegetable retailing.

4) Services Added to the Product Offering

Consider as an example of this, the 'You Ring, We Bring' delivery service being promoted by Office Works to increase its share of the highly competitive office supplies market.

Image Positioning

This type of positioning is that which is achieved merely on the basis of creating a specific 'image' of the product or service in the consumer's mind.

It is often employed by commodity marketers, where substantial differentiation is difficult to achieve or might not be worthwhile investing resources in.

In these and other instances where positioning is based on the creation of a strategic image of the product or service, it is primarily packaging and the elements of the marketing communications mix, such as advertising and promotions, that are used to achieve it.

In certain regards, perfume provides a prime example of image marketing. Whilst perfume manufacturers might present indignant arguments to the contrary, the stark reality is that perfume companies invest many millions of dollars in promoting just the right image for their fragrances, and in securing the services of famous actresses and other celebrities to create the right 'personalities' for them.

Group Exercise:

Identify and discuss examples of products or services positioned solely on a created image.

_____

_____

_____

_____

_____

_____

_____

_____

_____

_____

_____

_____

_____

_____

_____

_____

Identifying the Appropriate Positioning Strategy

In developing a positioning strategy, there are several considerations marketers must make, and specific research they must undertake.

These include:

1) Target Markets Selected

Again, the positioning strategy supports the target market selection. If, for example, a company wants to target a segment such as the hypothetical 'wealthy, outer-directed conspicuous consumer' mentioned in the section *Selecting the Target Segment or Segments*, it will need to ensure it can attain a suitably prominent and premium product positioning. Such an organisation will need to create a 'product with personality'.

2) Company Resources

For the most part, this assessment will have been made prior to an organisation making its selection of target market or markets. However, in developing a clear picture of the strategic positioning required for the product or service, there might well be additional considerations the organisation needs to make in terms of the resources it is capable of investing in the development, manufacture, distribution and promotion of its offering to that target market.

3) Existing Corporate or Brand Image

An organisation that already has a presence in the market must seriously consider its existing marketplace image. It must be realistic about any significantly different new positioning, with regard to the likelihood of changing consumer perceptions and/or the investment required to bring about the altered perception.

This might not be an issue for a multiple-segment player planning entry into a new market segment with a brand and marketing strategy distinct to the intended target market.

However, a single-segment marketer with an existing image in either that segment or another, wanting to inject a new product or service into the market with a substantially different positioning, should make this assessment carefully.

Group Exercise:

Identify and discuss either a product or a services company that failed in its bid to re-enter the market with a different brand image.

_____

_____

_____

_____

_____

_____

_____

_____

_____

_____

_____

_____

_____

_____

_____

_____

_____

Competitor Strategies

Competitors' strategies — both current and planned — should be the subject of keen investigation.

Competitors should be viewed in the broadest sense and nothing should be assumed or left to chance. Even the largest and most market-dominant organisations can have their competitive positioning encroached upon by, for example, a new entrant niche marketer with a canny feel for the market and changing trends.

Likewise, a company that has reverted to a product perspective of its offering, as opposed to constantly reviewing 'what business it's in', can find its market share knocked off by an alternative or substitute product that fills the same core need of consumers.

Alternatively, a better-resourced competitor might be planning an entry to the market with the same positioning statement and a stronger offering. An organisation's marketers need to be in possession of this type of knowledge. Here we straddle the issue of competitive intelligence, an emerging component in today's marketing strategies.

Questions For Marketers to Ask in Determining Market Positioning

When determining a USP or positioning statement, marketers should ask themselves the following series of questions:

- What are our inherent weaknesses and strengths as an organisation? (A SWOT — Strengths, Weaknesses, Opportunities and Threats — analysis should be undertaken.)

- What are the weaknesses and strengths of our product or service offering per se?

- What are our weaknesses and strengths in relation to the chosen target market or markets?

- In what ways are our product / service significantly different to our competitors'?

- Given the information resulting from the above, where does it make sense for us to position ourselves within the market, and with what Unique Selling Proposition?

- Is this market positioning compatible with our Corporate Mission Statement?

- What are the weaknesses and strengths of our competitors and their products or services?

- What are existing competitors within our chosen market segment or segments doing or intending to do?

- What potential new competition exists?

- What substitute or alternative products exist for the market segments we have chosen, and do any of these impact upon our desired positioning strategy?

- What are all the factors upon which our ability to attain and maintain the desired positioning is dependent?

- How long is this market position likely to be a profitable proposition? What societal or market trends are evident that might either erode or increase the desirability of this positioning strategy?

- Is the intended differentiation and positioning strategy viable?

- Is the intended differentiation and positioning strategy meaningful to those consumers comprising our chosen target market or markets?

This last question is critical. It also demonstrates the need for a detached and independent perspective by the organisation, as opposed to the common inward focus many companies demonstrate. Further, it underscores the need for authoritative research.

An organisation might consider its product's or service's competitive differences or USP far more significant than do its target customers.

A positioning statement must be based on a significant and meaningful difference over other available products and services or means of needs satisfaction.

Your Challenge (Individual):

Based on the individual challenge at the end of the section *Selecting the Target Segment or Segments* for your hypothetical product manufacturer, create a broader marketing scenario and provide written discussion on each of the above checklist questions.

_____
_____
_____
_____
_____
_____
_____
_____
_____
_____
_____
_____
_____

Marketing Mix Implications of Positioning Strategy

The positioning strategy affects every element of the marketing mix.

If the product or service is yet to be developed to suit the target market, the positioning strategy plays a critical role in this development phase. If external research is to be undertaken to guide development decisions, it will form the basis of the brief to the research company.

Packaging is an integral means of communicating all elements of a product's positioning strategy. In the services sector, the manner in which a firm's offerings are 'bundled' and presented is often dictated by the positioning strategy.

For example, a firm using is its comprehensive services offering as its USP, might choose to emphasise this positioning by offering its services as customisable 'packages', as opposed to focusing on individual products.

Distribution plays an equally pivotal role in supporting the positioning strategy. A product with an exclusive market positioning will not be credibly sold through a discount store network, for example.

For obvious reasons, pricing and payment terms will be a direct reflection of the positioning strategy.

And, of course, all elements of the marketing communications strategy (e.g. printed materials, point-of-sale material, advertising and promotions, along with publicity and other forms of public relations) will be designed to create the desired image for the product or service, as well as to reach its desired target markets both directly and indirectly.

Formulating the Positioning Strategy

The personal care and cosmetics industries provide a goldmine of examples of positioning — and repositioning — strategies.

Take the skincare brand Clinique. Clinique is clearly positioned for those who are serious about skincare. From its name, to its packaging, to the clinical-looking uniforms worn by the sales assistants staffing its department store counters — to say nothing of its pricing — Clinique's marketers have created an almost 'pharmaceutical' image.

This suggests certain strategies in relation to its target market, product differentiation and competitive positioning. In the cut-throat market of skincare, where brands usually rely on packaging, scientific-sounding product names, barely credible promises and models and personalities to differentiate themselves from their competitors, Clinique has arguably set itself apart, at least in terms of creating uniqueness of image.

Formulating the positioning strategy requires careful attention to all elements of the marketing mix.

For example, a company going after the 'premium quality' positioning within a marketplace must use that image to dictate every consideration involved in the development and production of that product, its packaging, its choice of distribution outlets, its back-up service, its customer-facing staff, and its advertising, promotions and other forms of marketing communications.

Case Study

Let's look at another real-life case as an example of how to formulate a competitive positioning statement.

One of the author's clients is a large provider of medical and rehabilitation services to injured workers. The organisation's actual client base comprises the employer companies. Its target market includes the general manufacturing sector.

The organisation's Unique Selling Proposition, or USP, revolves around its:

> *'Comprehensive range of integrated specialist medical, injury prevention and management services'.*

As a direct extension of this USP, its competitive Positioning Statement reads as follows:

> *'As the market's only provider of a comprehensive and integrated injury management services portfolio, we lead all competition – both direct and indirect – within the national marketplace.'*

Both concepts link back to that company's stated 'mission', which revolves around its commitment to the highest possible standards of medical care and rehabilitation service to the injured worker and a timely and safe return of that worker into the workplace, critical to which is its :

> *'Comprehensive range of integrated specialist medical, injury prevention and management services'.*

This organisation's management understands that these are no hollow statements, but vital performance standards to maintain its standing within its chosen marketplace.

Management therefore knows the organisation must retain the best medical specialists, rehabilitation personnel and customer-facing staff. It knows it must retain the best-equipped fleet of emergency vehicles.

It knows it must maintain excellent employee and employer communications and reporting systems. And it knows the presentation of its buildings, staff, vehicles and marketing materials must be in keeping with the premium positioning it has chosen to occupy within its marketplace.

Customer Groups Within Customer Groups

When formulating a positioning strategy and statement, be mindful that, in the case of many products and services, different 'audiences' play a role in the purchase decision and ultimate consumption of that product or service (refer back to the section *Audiences within Market Segments*). Remember that these audiences can include:

- Influencers
- Decision makers
- Purchasers
- Ultimate consumers.

In formulating the positioning strategy, it is essential for marketers to understand the role played by each.

Assignment:

(Individual)

On your next supermarket visit, select a product category and either collect, or make notes on, the packaging of several different brands with regard to the positioning of each, within that category. Alternatively, using the above case example for guidance, select a large, household-name service firm, and notate your thoughts on its positioning strategy, including the elements of its marketing mix that support its positioning.

(Group)

In your next class session, compare notes by each member of the class.

Your Challenge (Individual):

Select a large consumer goods company or a high-profile service firm with a multiple-segment strategy. Visit its website to determine whether it features reasonably detailed information about the brands / products / services it competes in the different market segments with. (If it doesn't, keep surfing until you find one that does.) Produce a basic analysis of your selected organisation's positioning strategy within each segment.

_____

_____

_____

_____

_____

_____

_____

_____

_____

_____

_____

_____

_____

Section 6:
Putting It All Together

Let's review what we've learned together in this module on market segmentation, target market selection, target marketing strategy and competitive positioning.

The Role of Marketing

Firstly, we have seen that marketing has not only a *broad* role, but also an *all-encompassing* role, within the organisation. Employed optimally, its influence begins *before* the creation of the product, service, event, cause or concept, and *extends past* even the ultimate point of sale.

Identifying the Overall Market

We have developed a close appreciation of the importance of beginning the marketing process with a clear picture of the overall marketplace. Further, we understand the critical nature of carefully analysing the total market in order to identify the segments of that market which are within the organisation's capacity to service, are the most profitable, and are the most strategically aligned with its corporate objectives.

Segmenting the Market

We have learned the key methodology by which to carry out this identification and segmentation process, according to geography, demographics, psychographics and purchasing behaviour, and the range of variables within each.

These variables include, in the case of *geographic* segmentation — country, state, region or city, population, population density and climate.

In the case of *demographics* — age group, gender, income or wealth status, social class, nationality, family size and life stage, education level, occupation and religion.

In the case of *psychographics* — lifestyle, values, personality and influences. In the case of *behavioural* segmentation — actual needs, benefits sought, purchase occasion, frequency of purchase or use; user status, loyalty status, product and purchase attitude, brand attitude and degree of convincing or information required to bring about purchase and use of the product or service.

We have seen how, in most cases, these different sets of variables converge in the identification of useful and authoritative market segments. We then studied the manner in which, for ease of communication within the organisation, marketers create working names for the various segments of their overall marketplaces.

Qualifying Market Segments

In order to qualify any particular subset of the market as a 'segment' for possible consideration as a target market, we identified that it must be *measurable, identifiable, accessible, substantial, distinguishable, homogenous, stable* and *practical to service*.

Further still, we learned that, in some cases, there are additional, corporate considerations in both identifying potentially serviceable market segments and selecting target markets. Amongst other factors, these include compatibility with the organisation's corporate and growth goals, consistency with the corporate image or desired corporate image, the strategies of competitors, and the cost of entry into the market segment/s in question.

We learned too, the importance of determining the various 'customer groups within customer groups' i.e. influencers, decision makers, purchasers and ultimate consumers, along with examples of their roles in the purchasing and consumption process.

Market and Competitor Information

We identified the different categories of market-related information likely to be required by an organisation in the process of segmenting its overall marketplace and selecting target markets. In answer to these requirements, we have discovered a wide range of both primary and secondary sources of this information.

Targeting Strategies

After learning how markets are segmented and target markets selected, we discovered and studied the four basic target market selection strategies available to marketers i.e. *mass*, *single-segment*, *multiple-segment* and *niche marketing*. Looking at the advantages and disadvantages of each, we then discussed in what set of circumstances a product or service marketer might choose the different approaches.

We then looked at aligning the selection of a target market strategy with an organisation's unique requirements.

Profiling Target Markets

We moved on to produce specific profiles of our selected target markets, and to become familiar with the terminology concepts employed by marketers. These include creating their own memorable, self-descriptive names for the market segments. Usually, these reflect the convergence of their chosen set of segmentation variables.

The Positioning Strategy

Ultimately, we arrived at the development of a positioning strategy. Linked directly to the organisation's *Unique Selling Proposition (USP)*, this involves determining the *competitive position* its product or service will occupy within the chosen target market segments. We discovered how, invariably, an organisation not definitive and proactive in identifying its USP or establishing and maintaining a positioning strategy, would be forced into the least desirable position within its market, whilst others enjoy the best competitive positions.

Product and Service Differentiation

We investigated the areas in which an organisation's offering can be differentiated, in order to achieve a Unique Selling Proposition (USP) and competitive position in the marketplace. These might include, in the case of a product — *quality, features, benefits, price, performance, style* and *environmental friendliness*; and, in the case of a service — *guarantees, technical support, standards of service, convenience* and *additional services* to the core service.

'Image Positioning'

We discussed the concept of 'image positioning', observing instances in which differentiation is achieved through brand image alone.

It is important, however, that this not be confused with differentiation based on the promise of a tangible point of difference or superiority. Where this is the case, the marketing mix must be set to deliver on such promises.

Aligning Strategy with Objectives

We learned how to identify an organisation's most appropriate positioning strategy, taking into account considerations such as the *target markets* selected, *company resources*, *existing corporate or brand image* and *competitor strategies.* We learned the questions that can be asked to help determine a positioning strategy and to verify the logic of that decision.

We considered the marketing mix implications of the positioning strategy, and the importance of every element of the marketing mix being formulated to support that market positioning.

Finally, we undertook the actual formulation of the positioning strategy.

A specific case example illustrated for us the fact that an organisation's positioning strategy is a direct extrapolation of its USP. In turn, we saw that both are based firmly upon the organisation's actual mission, preferably as conveyed in an actual corporate Mission Statement (the responsibility of top-level management and the organisation's board of directors).

Aligning Marketing Mix with Strategy

Our observations left us with the conviction that marketing management should not treat either the USP or the competitive positioning statement as simply promotional catchcries. As future business owners, managers or marketing managers, we saw clearly that our organisations and their products and services must live up to the desired reputation in every aspect of production, operations and marketing.

The ultimate role of the marketing mix is, in fact, to directly support the Unique Selling Proposition and the positioning strategy adopted by the organisation for its marketplace offering.

The 'Big Picture'

And so we learned not only the importance of, but also the inherent relationship between, *market identification*, *segmentation*, *target market* selection, *profiling* and *strategy decision*, and *positioning strategy* formulation.

Of course, we also learned to adapt and apply these marketing principles to business and industrial markets. We learned, in these instances, to identify the special considerations involved in identifying, selecting and profiling markets for industrial or business-to-business products and services, in order to ensure this type of offering is positioned optimally within the chosen market segments.

Your Ultimate Challenge:

Select :

(a)   a nationally or internationally-known brand-name consumer product;

(b)   a well-known services marketer within the national or international consumer marketplace, and

(c)   a high-profile business-to-business or industrial product or service marketer.

Using any appropriate sources of information from those listed in the section *Sources of Market Information*, determine and discuss in writing, the decisions made and strategies selected for the marketing of each product and service with regard to its:

- overall marketplace

- marketplace segmentation and the likely methodology and variables used

- target market/s selection

- target market/s approach strategy

- specific target market profiles

- product or service differentiation

- USP

- competitive positioning strategy

- alignment between (a) its USP and market positioning strategy, and (b) the various elements of its marketing mix.

> **Hint:** Collect recent examples of the various advertising campaigns run by your chosen companies, as a starting point in helping you determine each of the above.

_____

_____

_____

_____

_____

_____

_____

_____

_____

_____

_____

_____

_____

_____

_____

_____

_____

_____